100 Afro-mations for Black Children

100 Afro-mations for Black Children

In a language they can understand

Malik Wright

Malik Wright

To the children,

I know what it feels like to have that long list of things you hate about life.

Don't let yourself fall on that list.

Love, Mr. Sandwich

Foreword

One of the reasons I made the decision to create this book is to directly address an observable social discrepancy between people of varying cultures. Another reason is to pass along the powerful treasure of affirmations. This will facilitate the healing of the minds and hearts of the youth; whom I identify with, and are a part of my community.

Throughout my life, I have been immersed in, internalizing, and molded by Black and African-American values, attitudes, languages and artistry. It is by far the most prominent contributing factor to the human that I am today. As I have been growing, I've been able to introduce and learn from many other cultures around the world. One of the social discrepancies I have directly observed exists in verbal communication. Many people do not understand particular words, phrases and grammar that are most familiar to me and the people nearest to me. There is a sentiment that may not be outwardly expressed but is subtly received in that the things that myself and others choose to say and the way in which we say them imply a level of intellectual inadequacy. That how we talk doesn't make sense. This is not the case. And this is what I'm here to address.

Nearly every major language in the world has subsects that are cultural renditions of the mother tongue. Spanish in Spain is different from Spanish in Mexico and Spanish in Colombia. This is the case for many Black and African-American communities and households with English. The lingo and grammar may not be what the authors of English textbooks, and tutors are deeming correct, but I'm here to reinforce the truth that it don't matter what anyone is "deeming". This dialect,

Foreword

African-American Vernacular English, is actively existing, evolving, being passed down and most importantly UNDERSTOOD; and a rendition of a language does not negate the presence of logical and meaningful thought. You might not get it but that does not mean that you can't. Feel free to ask for clarity. That's the most intelligent thing to do. This goes for all people of the world, not just people who do not understand when a black woman says "It's giving what needs to be gave" or a black man says "It's no cap in my rap". We all can learn from one another and come together for a more honest and respectful understanding of each other's existence. 'Cus most folks be knowing what they getting at and I'ont think you wanna be the one looking like a goofy for not asking.

Along with addressing the disconnect I've experienced with the language of my global community, I created this book because of what affirmations have done and are still doing for my healing. Affirmations have been one of the most psychologically therapeutic instruments I have learned in my life. There is power in reading, in thoughts and in the tongue. Experiencing various severe traumas in my life had me in an extremely stagnant, hateful and pessimistic place for a long time. I had given up on myself and everyday was a debilitating sadness. I felt trapped. The power in the words I was using was working against me. I was beating myself up over everything I did and it got uncontrollable and very dark. It wasn't until I started getting therapy that I was suggested exposure to affirmations to combat the self-destructive habits and thought patterns that were killing my self-esteem and life satisfaction. It took me a minute to get around to incorporating them more regularly in my day-to-day life.

One day I followed an account on Instagram (@affirmations) and it was like a light cut on in my brain. Every day I would read through these short messages and I could feel the stress leaving my mind. I could feel the lightening up of my thoughts and it was beautiful. I started agreeing with beauty and greatness. I said to myself, 'I could have used this an incredibly long time ago', and that's when the idea hit me. I know I could have used this when I was younger, so I'm going to create something so that the children after me, who may feel the same way I did, don't have to deal with what I was dealing with. I wanted it to speak to the experiences of as many Black and African American youth as possible so I made sure to incorporate as many of the meaningful,

Foreword

relevant and unique phrases and terminologies from all of the people and communities that I have learned from and been influenced by. You will see representations from Atlanta, New York, the DMV, California, Pittsburgh, Chicago and even the Caribbean/West Indies. This is a product of the Global Black Community. Once again, there may be phrases here that you may not be familiar with or have different meanings for, but all that creates is an opportunity to learn what they mean and where they come from. So it's a lowkey win-win sichee-ayeshun.

In many ways, what I have created here is a weapon against self-destruction for the children out there that will grow up to be greater than I am. Use it. Internalize it. Embrace it. Apply it and SHARE it to those that may need it. Remember: Keep fighting without your fists!!!

I love you and you will too.

Ya feel me?

#1

I won't ever let anyone or anything control me. I am free.

2

I don't participate in gossip. If it ain't got nothing to do with me then I'm staying out of it.

#3

I'm not a watcher or a waiter. I'm a doer.

#4

When I want something to happen, I make it happen myself.

#5

I'm always thinking and planning ahead. Y'all ain't finna catch me slipping moe.

#6

I love myself because I know myself.

#7

I'm glowing up and gone keep glowing up forever so I suggest y'all stay out the way.

#8

I'm really lit out here. Like… in real life.

#9

If anyone tries to control me or make me feel bad about myself, they will be let down and subsequently embarrassed.

#10

I never stop striving for better and because of that, better will always find me.

Actions speak louder than words. I believe what people do and not what they say.

#12

I think before I act, so when I'm doing something best believe I'm sure about it.

#13

Excuse me, is you saying something?... Unh-Unh, you can't tell me NOTHING.

#14

Just because I don't feel like talking does not mean I'm being rude. I don't feel like talking all the time and that will be respected. I don't owe a single soul my conversation.

15

I am a defense mechanism against insecurity and hatred.

#16

Some things will never go out of style. I am one of them.

#17

My overcoming is ongoing. There is no such thing as an insurmountable obstacle to me.

#18

I will never allow myself to be crippled by fear. I am courageous and will overcome everything that tries to scare me.

#19

I feel confident in myself when I'm doing the things I love, and I'm always doing the things I love.

#20

When something needs to happen, I'm always finding a way to make it happen.

#21

I don't carry stress. I eliminate stress.

#22

My life belongs to me and only me. I ain't ever giving it away.

#23

I'm living my best life. I ain't going back and forth with you haters.

#24

If I'm passionate about it, there ain't nothing that can keep me from it.

#25

I'm real deal in tune with my heart, my brain, my body and everything around me. I always know how I feel even if I can't find the words for it.

#26

Sometimes I be feeling anxious when I'm around people. However, I always find my peace knowing that most folks ain't even stunting me to begin with.

#27

I have the power to make my life look however I want this thang to look.

#28

Once I know better, I do better. I don't make the same mistakes twice.

#29

The smarter I get, the easier my life is.

#30

I'm better than I was yesterday. No kizzy.

31

I'm here to provide a little bit of straightening.

#32

I don't allow myself to get too happy or too sad. I stay balanced and centered so life doesn't catch me off guard.

#33

I don't too much care about material things. Happiness, rest, confidence and freedom are much more valuable things to have.

#34

I don't always like everything about myself and that's a'ight. I work on those things and I will learn to love them too.

#35

I love myself enough to always make sure I'm happy and my needs are being met.

#36

I love myself, my body, my mind and my heart so much.

#37

I'm beautiful because I refuse to hate on anyone no matter what.

#38

I'm beautiful because of the beauty that I create.

#39

I ain't judging people that I don't even know like that. No ma'am, no sir.

… #40

Talking to myself be helping me make sense out of the things I'm going through.

#41

It is what it is and gone be what it be.

#42

If people don't like me when I tell the truth then that's on them. I'm gone tell it regardless. I will not live a lie.

#43

Mi run tings, tings nuh run mi.

#44

I'm not gone see eye to eye with everybody and that's just fine. It ain't my job to do that anyway.

#45

I won't let people get me tight. I always end my day on chill time.

#46

I carry my confidence with me everywhere I go.

#47

Sometimes I just wanna be left alone and vibe in my room. I deserve some time to myself.

#48

I be enjoying the simple things that life has to offer like sunlight and birds chirping.

#49

I tend to cut out the extra and get straight to the point.

#50

I'm not crazy or angry when I stand up for myself. Y'all just not about to play with me.

#51

I do not advocate for violence but I will use it to defend myself if it go like that.

#52

I choose to love on everybody because that's who I am by nature. However, that don't mean I won't slap fire out of somebody if I need to. I am peaceful, not harmless.

#53

I refuse to hate myself for any reason whatsoever. It ain't finna go down like that.

#54

I will never allow anyone's bad energy to rub off on me.

#55

I won't ever forget how it feels to love on myself. That feeling will live with me forever.

#56

When I'm down bad, I don't allow myself to get stuck there. Trouble don't last always.

#57

I love myself too much to go out sad.

#58

Unfortunately for all my haters, my future will be getting brighter.

#59

I don't allow anyone from anywhere to mistreat me. All disrespect gets checked.

#60

The voice in my head tells me to love myself more.

#61

I am confident and I radiate confidence.

62

I am an easy-going spirit just don't walk up on me wrong.

#63

I don't wear the drip, I am the drip.

#64

Resting is important to me. When I am well-rested, everything goes much better.

#65

Some days don't be hitting the way I want them to but I know it ain't always going to be perfect. That's life.

#66

My greatness is not a fluke. When I do something dope, best believe I can and will do it again. I'm not lucky, I just got skills boi.

#67

Today Ima look out for me first.

#68

Today Ima laugh and feel the joy.

#69

Seeing my people happy really be doing something to me.

#70

When I'm feeling some type of way about something, I speak up and change it.

#71

No matter what clothes I wear, my confidence is never fading. It's in me, not on me.

#72

All self-hating thoughts I may experience are ova wit. Ima live it up until I'm done.

#73

On God y'all can't kill my vibe.

#74

Nephs my friends unique and solid.

… #75

On foe nem my day will be decent.

#76

I am not OD.

#77

I do not cap to myself or to others.

#78

I do not tolerate cap from myself or from others.

#79

I know how to explain myself.

#80

I am not an enabler of anything goofy.

#81

I am not an enabler of any weirdo behaviors.

#82

I am not a Buford.

#83

I am not a bozo.

#84

I'm putting in the work on the front end so when the opportunities present themselves I can show out.

#85

I'm not for none of that talking. I show better than I tell.

#86

People will get everything they deserve at the end of the day. Good, bad and in between.

#87

**I be on one when I see people happy.
I like making people happy.**

#88

Sometimes people don't deserve my time. And I'm just fine with leaving them be. Love from a distance is a healthy practice to have.

#89

I will never let what folks say or feel about what I do, keep me from doing it. I like what I like. Period.

#90

I'm me. I do me, and I chill.

#91

Sometimes my teachers be tripping on me but that ain't gone stop me from learning. Ima get my education.

#92

I love myself and there ain't a single thing anybody can do about it.

#93

Life can be really hard sometimes but I'm not gonna quit. I have to figure this thing out.

#94

I pull inspiration from the people around me, but at the end of the day I do things in my own unique way. I am one of one.

#95

Some of my peers might try to get me to do stuff that don't make sense and I promise you I'm not going for none of it.

#96

I don't be stunting what other folks got going on. I mind my business and stay to myself.

#97

I know I be tripping sometimes but at the end of the day I just want everybody to win. Myself included.

#98

Some days everything just be funny and it ain't nothing wrong about being in a good mood.

#99

I really appreciate the folks that do right by me.

#100

The folks that don't do right by me will never get an opportunity to do it again and that's on everything I love.

Affectionately known by his students as "Mr. Sandwich", Malik Wright is a lover of art, music, laughing, food, animals and nature. He is a self-love and mental health advocate and believes in the power of words on the heart and the mind. He still resides on Earth where he is the world's greatest substitute teacher and wants all of his readers to remember:

Wu-Tang is for the children.

www.ingramcontent.com/pod-product-compliance
Lightning Source LLC
Chambersburg PA
CBHW051213290426
44109CB00021B/2438